JOHN RUTTER
MISSA BREVIS

FOR SATB CHOIR AND ORGAN

OXFORD

OXFORD
UNIVERSITY PRESS

Great Clarendon Street, Oxford OX2 6DP,
United Kingdom

Oxford University Press is a department of the University of Oxford.
It furthers the University's objective of excellence in research, scholarship,
and education by publishing worldwide. Oxford is a registered trade mark of
Oxford University Press in the UK and in certain other countries

First published 2022

Impression: 1

ISBN 978–0–19–356245–5

Music originated on Sibelius
Printed in Great Britain on acid-free paper by
Halstan & Co. Ltd, Amersham, Bucks.

Composed at the invitation of the Chapter of York in memory of Richard Shephard,
and first performed in York Minster on 11 July 2021 by the boy choristers and adult singers of the Minster Choir,
directed by Robert Sharpe.

MISSA BREVIS

JOHN RUTTER

I. Kyrie

John Rutter's organ piece *Celebration* was written to follow the Missa Brevis as an outgoing voluntary. It is published separately by Oxford University Press (ISBN 978-019-3562349).

*The small notes are alternatives.

8

II. Gloria

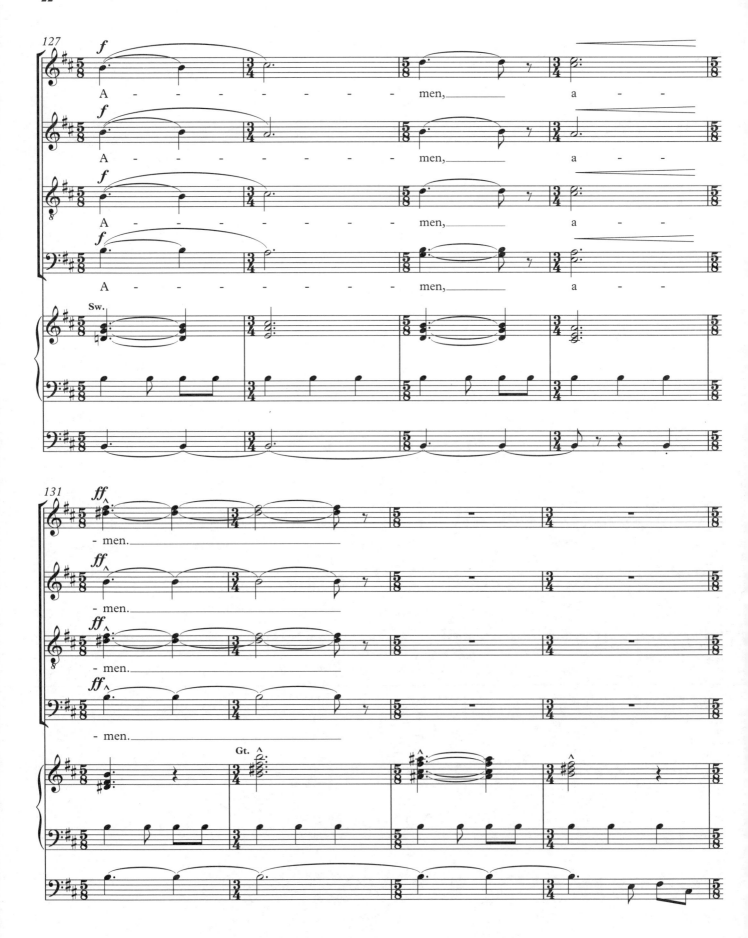

III. Sanctus

*Choice of manuals at organist's discretion.

IV. Benedictus

V. Agnus Dei

rallentando al fine